My Feelings

By

Grace Jones

©2017
Book Life
King's Lynn
Norfolk PE30 4LS

ISBN: 978-1-78637-109-6

Written by:
Grace Jones

Designed by:
Danielle Jones

A catalogue record for this book
is available from the British Library

Photo Credits

**Abbreviations: l-left, r-right, b-bottom,
t-top, c-centre, m-middle.**

Front cover – . 2 – michaeljung 4 – windu. 5– Ermolaev Alexander.
6 – Luis Molinero. 7l – Melissa King 7m – holbox. 7r – Vinicius Tupinamba.
8 – Tatyana Vyc. 9 – Oksana Kuzmina. 10 – Oksana Kuzmina. 11 – Robert
Kneschke. 12 – bbevren. 13 – BestPhotoStudio. 14 – Fotomay. 15 – Ilike.
16 – vesna cvorovic. 17 – Kiselev Andrey Valerevich. 18 – wavebreakmediav.
19 – varandah. 20 – varandah. 21 – Khakimullin Aleksandr. 22 – Suzanne Tucker.
23 – Marina Dyakonova.
Images are courtesy of Shutterstock.com. With thanks to Getty Images,
Thinkstock Photo and iStockphoto.

Contents

Words that look like **this** can be found in the glossary on page 24.

What are Feelings?

Do you feel happy, sad, angry, scared, shy or worried? These are all feelings.

Sad

Worried

A person can have many different feelings.

Your feelings don't stay the same all the time.

Can you tell how each of these children are feeling?

It is important to talk about how you feel.

Happy

Happy

When you are happy, you feel good about yourself.

Feeling happy can make you feel **brave** and **confident**.

Sometimes other people do things to make you happy.

Other times you might feel happy if you do well at something at school or at home.

Sad

Sad

Lots of different things can make you sad.

Feeling sad can make you very upset and can even make you cry.

13

When I lost my teddy, I felt sad.

Sometimes other people do things that can make you sad.

Other times you might feel sad if you can't play with your friends.

Angry

You can get angry for lots of different reasons.

You might be angry with yourself or at someone else.

You might get angry if you think your mum or dad are not being **fair**.

Other times you might feel angry if someone hurts or annoys you.

19

Scared

Scared

When you are scared, you feel **frightened** about someone or something.

20

You might be scared of sleeping in the dark.

You might try and hide from someone or something that scares you.

Remember, it's always best to speak to your mum or dad if you feel scared.

Glossary

brave   not afraid

confident   feeling that you can do something well

fair   treating people the same

frightened afraid or worried

Index